Let's Make MUSIC

The Violin
and Other Stringed Instruments

Rita Storey

A⁺

Smart Apple Media

Smart Apple Media
P.O. Box 3263, Mankato, Minnesota 56002

Printed in the United States

Published by arrangement with the Watts Publishing Group Ltd, London.

Art director: Jonathan Hair
Series designed and created for Franklin Watts by Painted Fish Ltd.
Designer: Rita Storey
Editor: Fiona Corbridge
Advisor: Helen MacGregor

Picture credits
istockphoto.com pp. 6, 9, 10, 11(bottom), 18, 19, 21–23, 25 and 26; Andrew
Lepley/Redferns p. 25; David Redfern/Redferns p. 22; Tudor Photography pp. 3, 7,
8, 11 (top), 12, 13, 14, 15, 16, 17, 20; Ulster Orchestra p. 24.

Cover images: Tudor Photography, Banbury (top); istock.com (bottom).

All photos posed by models.
Thanks to Husnen Ahmad, James Barlow, Maddi Indun, Mary Martin, Stephen
Morris, Jack Phillips, George Stapleton, and Natasha Vinall.

Library of Congress Cataloging-in-Publication Data

Storey, Rita.
  The violin and other stringed instruments / by Rita Storey.
      p. cm. -- (Let's make music)
  Includes index.
  Summary: "Introduces the violin and other stringed instruments, such as the
guitar and cello, and explains which musical instruments are used to form
certain musical groups"--Provided by publisher.
  ISBN 978-1-59920-212-9 (hardcover)
  1. Stringed instruments--Juvenile literature. I. Title.
  ML750.S72 2010
  787--dc22
                              2008039685

Contents

Words in **bold** are in the glossary.

The Violin

A violin is a musical instrument with four strings. To make music with it, draw the bow across the strings or pluck them with your fingers.

A violin is made of wood. A bow is made of wood and horsehair.

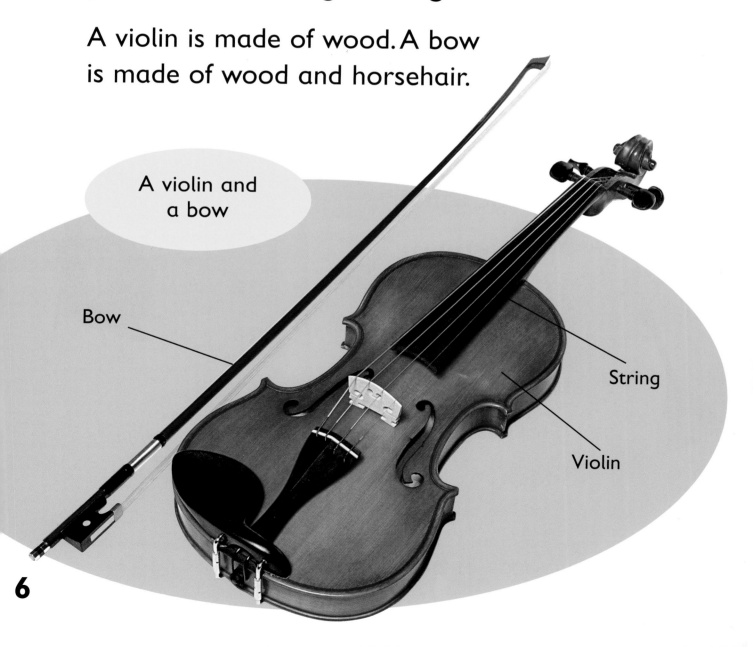

A violin and a bow

Bow

String

Violin

How to Play

To play a violin, tuck it between your chin and shoulder. Hold the bow in your other hand.

Making a Sound

When you move the hair of the bow back and forth against the strings of the violin, it makes sounds.

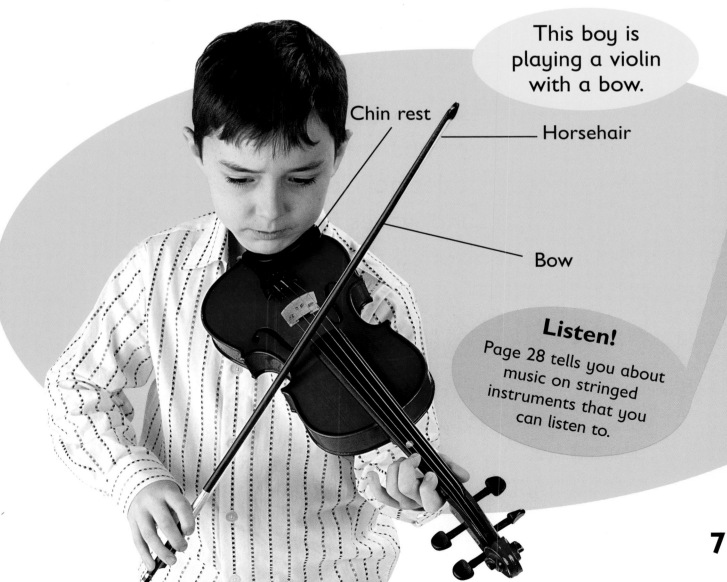

Chin rest

This boy is playing a violin with a bow.

Horsehair

Bow

Listen!
Page 28 tells you about music on stringed instruments that you can listen to.

7

The Sound

When you play a string on a musical instrument, it shakes very fast. The string is vibrating.

Moving the Air

When the string **vibrates**, it makes the air around it move. The way the air moves is called a **sound wave**.

Making Waves

Stretch a rubber band over your fingers. Pull it gently and let go. Can you see it vibrate? The sound waves from the elastic band made the sound that you heard.

Getting Louder

On a violin, the strings are stretched across a piece of wood called a bridge.

When you play the strings, the **vibrations** go down the bridge into the hollow body of the violin. The sound gets louder and comes out through the sound holes.

Wooden bridge

Strings stretched over the bridge

These sound holes let the sound escape from inside the violin.

Hollow body

The Strings

Each of the four strings on a violin makes a different sound, or musical note, when you play it.

These four notes on their own would not be enough to make interesting music. There are ways to make many different notes on a stringed instrument.

The thickest string makes the lowest note.

The thinnest string makes the highest note.

High and Low

Some musical notes are high and some are low. We call this their **pitch**.

If you make a string shorter, it will make a higher note. You can do this by pressing your finger on it.

Another way to make a higher note is to make the string tighter.

Tuning

Before you start to play, you must check that each string plays the correct note. This is called tuning.

You tune a violin by turning the tuning pegs.

Tuning pegs

Playing Notes

If you press the bow hard on the strings, the sound will be loud. If you press gently, the sound will be quieter.

Playing Pizzicato

Sometimes you play a violin by plucking the strings with your fingers. This is called **pizzicato**. It sounds very different than when you use a bow.

Playing a violin pizzicato

Long and Short

To play a note that lasts a long time, use the whole length of the bow. For a short note, take the bow off the string quickly.

Music Notes

To be able to play music that other people have made up, or composed, you need to understand how to read music.

Music is written in musical notes. There are **symbols** to tell us how long or short a note is. The length of the notes make up the **rhythm** of a piece of music.

The notes are written on five lines called a staff. The place of a note on the staff tells us how high or low it is. This is called its pitch.

A long note   A short note   A low note   A high note

This girl is playing a long note.

Different Sizes

Here are more stringed instruments that are played with a bow. The bigger the instrument is, the deeper the sound it makes.

The Violin and Viola

A violin has a high pitch. A viola is bigger than a violin and has a lower pitch. These instruments can be played standing up or sitting down. They are held under the chin.

Viola

Violin

The Cello

This is much bigger than a viola and has a deeper pitch. The player sits down to play it and holds it between her knees.

Double bass

Cello

The Double Bass

This is the largest stringed instrument played with a bow. It has a very low pitch. The player sits on a high stool and rests the double bass between his knees.

The Guitar

The guitar is a stringed instrument too. To make music with it, you strum the strings with your fingers or pluck them with a piece of plastic called a pick.

Playing a guitar with a pick

Picks come in different colors and patterns.

Strumming a guitar

How to Play

To hold a guitar, put the body under one arm and support the neck with your other hand. To play, hold down the strings on the fingerboard in different places and strum.

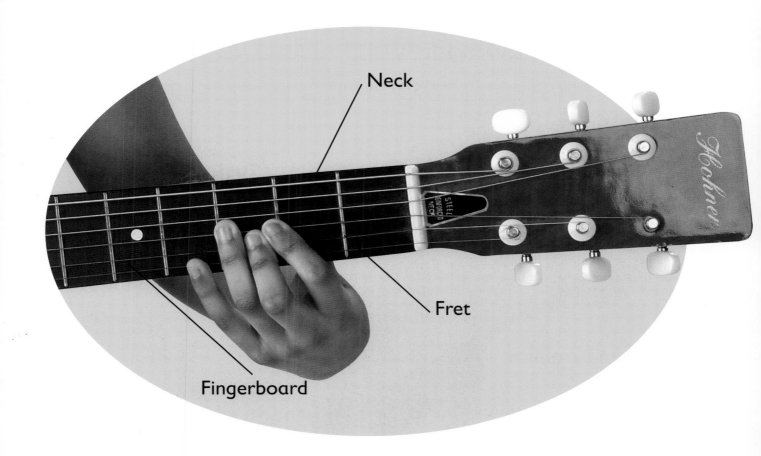

Neck

Fret

Fingerboard

The fingerboard has pieces of metal on it that divide it into sections. These are called frets. The frets help show you where to put your fingers to change the notes.

Acoustic Guitar

There are two kinds of guitars—acoustic and electric.

An **acoustic** guitar is made of wood. It has a hollow body, which makes the sound louder in the same way as a violin (see page 9).

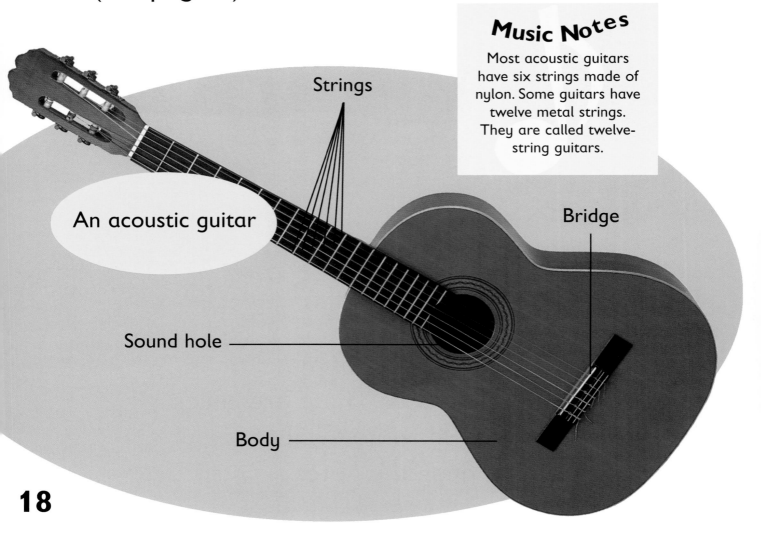

Strings

Music Notes

Most acoustic guitars have six strings made of nylon. Some guitars have twelve metal strings. They are called twelve-string guitars.

An acoustic guitar

Bridge

Sound hole

Body

Spanish Guitar

The acoustic guitar is sometimes called the Spanish guitar because it is used to play Spanish music called flamenco.

Stamp Your Feet

There are special dances for flamenco music. Flamenco dancers stamp their feet and clap their hands as part of the dance.

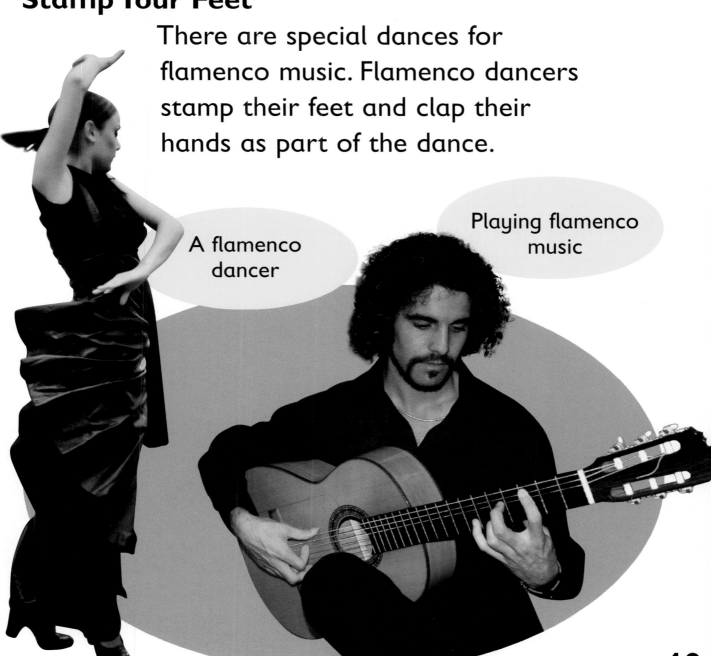

A flamenco dancer

Playing flamenco music

Electric Guitar

An electric guitar has metal strings and is made of solid wood. It needs electricity to make it work.

Strings

Most electric guitars have six metal strings.

Electric bass guitars have four strings and a very low pitch.

An electric guitar

Strings

Pickups

Controls for changing **volume** and **tone**

Cord that plugs into the **amplifier**

Loud Noise

An electric guitar has pickups under the strings.

The pickups turn the vibrations from the strings into sound by using an amplifier that stands on the floor. The sound comes out through a **loudspeaker**.

Rock and Pop Music

Electric guitars are popular with pop and rock groups. Music groups usually have at least one guitar and a bass guitar.

Music Notes

The volume of an electric guitar can be turned up and down.
It can be made much louder than the volume of an acoustic guitar.

Cord

Small practice amplifier

Loudspeaker

More Strings

Many different types of stringed instruments are played in countries all over the world. Here are just a few of them.

Kora
The kora comes from West Africa. It is made from the hollowed-out shell of a fruit called a gourd.

Sitar
The sitar comes from South Asia. It has about 20 metal strings. It can be over 3 feet (1 m) long.

Bouzouki
This instrument comes from Greece. It is played with a pick and has a metallic sound.

Balalaika
This instrument is from Russia. It is shaped like a triangle and comes in six different sizes. Musicians play folk music on it. There are also balalaika **orchestras**.

23

The Orchestra

An orchestra is a large number of musicians who play together.

The largest type of orchestra is a **symphony** orchestra. It has about one hundred musicians.

Stringed instruments make up over half of a symphony orchestra.

Can you name the stringed instruments in this orchestra?

The Harp

A harp is sometimes part of the string section of an orchestra. It stands on the floor and you play it by plucking the strings with your fingers.

A harp has forty-seven strings.

Playing Together

Smaller groups of musicians also play together. This group of four people has two violins, a viola, and a cello. They are called a string quartet.

A string quartet

Express Yourself

There is much more to music than just playing notes. Stringed instruments can sound very different if they are played in different ways.

Feelings

Music can change how you feel—it can make you feel happy or sad, calm or excited. It might be very loud and thrilling, or quiet and peaceful.

This guitarist is playing loud rock music.

This guitarist is playing a bass guitar in a **jazz** band.

Music Notes

The speed at which a piece of music is played is called its **tempo**.

Listen!

Web Sites

Stringed Instruments

Explore the orchestra with the New York Philharmonic. Take a walk through the instrument storage room with different cartoon guides. Play fun games like Instrument Frenzy, where you need to sort out the instruments before a concert. Go to:
http://www.nyphilkids.org

Take a tour of the virtual orchestra room and see the string instruments the Dallas Symphony uses. Click on the seating chart and find which instrument is placed in what spot. Go to:
www.dsokids.com/

Click on the string section of the orchestra to listen to each instrument, including the harp, at the children's website of the San Francisco Symphony Orchestra:
www.sfskids.org/templates/instorchframe.asp?pageid=3

Guitar

See video of flamenco guitarists, including Juan Diego, at:
www.flamenco-world.com/video/videos_guitar.htm

Read an interview with a jazz guitarist (who started playing when he was six years old) and listen to his music at:
www.jazzguitar.be/jazz_guitar_free_mp3_chris_standring.html

Sitar

Meet Anoushka Shankar, a famous sitar player since the age of 13. Learn about her family history with the sitar instrument and watch an interview where she talks about making a music album:
www.anoushkashankar.com

Listen to more sitar music at:
www.biswabratachakrabarti.com/english/audio/audio.html

Kora

Hear Mamadou Diabate, the famous kora player from Mali in West Africa, at: *www.mamadoukora.com/*

See photos of koras being made at a Gambian kora workshop at: *www.coraconnection.com/flash/index.html*

Visit Sound Junction, at the Associated Board of the Royal Schools of Music, to learn more about the kora and hear kora music at: *www.soundjunction.org/Allaboutthekora.aspa*

Balalaika

See photos, watch video and download mp3 files of balalaika music at: *www.barynya.com/balalaika.htm*

Bouzouki

Watch videos of different bouzouki players at: *www.mpouzouki.com*

CDs

Listen to these well-known pieces of orchestral music to hear the strings:

Edward Elgar: *Serenade for Strings*—"Introduction and Allegro".
Benjamin Britten: *Simple Symphony*.
Camille Saint-Saëns: *Danse Macabre* (violin). *Carnival of the Animals*—"The Swan" (cello); "The Elephant" (double bass).
Pyotr Tchaikovsky: *Swan Lake*—"Swans" (no. 13) (violins). *Nutcracker*—"Waltz of the Flowers" (harp).
Vaughan Williams: *Lark Ascending* (violin).

Listen to these examples of bouzouki music:

Iordanis Tsomidis: *The Music of Greece*.
Michalis Terzis: *Magic of the Greek Bouzouki*.

Glossary

Acoustic Describes an instrument that does not use electricity to produce sound.

Amplifier A piece of equipment for increasing the strength of a sound.

Jazz A style of music that began in New Orleans, USA, around the beginning of the twentieth century.

Loudspeaker A device for changing electrical signals into sounds that we can hear.

Orchestra A large group of performers playing various musical instruments.

Pitch A high musical note or sound is said to have a high pitch. A low musical note or sound is said to have a low pitch.

Pizzicato A way of playing strings by plucking them with the fingers instead of using a bow.

Rhythm The regular pattern of sound in music.

Sound wave A wave that transmits sound through the air.

Strumming Playing a stringed instrument by running your fingers lightly across the strings.

Symbol A shape or image used to represent something else.

Symphony A long piece of instrumental music written for a big orchestra.

Tempo The speed at which music is played.

Tone The quality of a sound. For example, it could be sharp or soft.

Vibrates; vibration Moving back and forth rapidly.

Volume The strength of a sound: it can be loud or quiet.

Index